The Magic School Bus

Explores Human Evolution

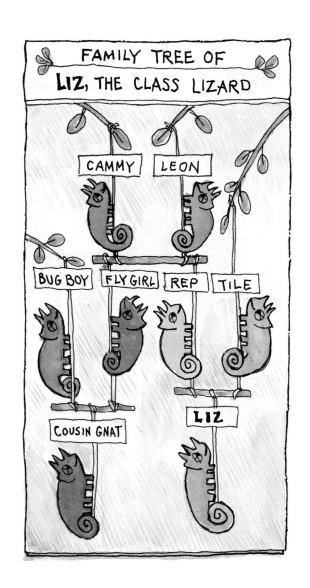

FAMILY TREE OF
LIZ, THE CLASS LIZARD

CAMMY   LEON

BUG BOY   FLY GIRL   REP   TILE

COUSIN GNAT   LIZ

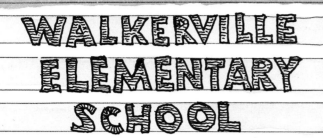

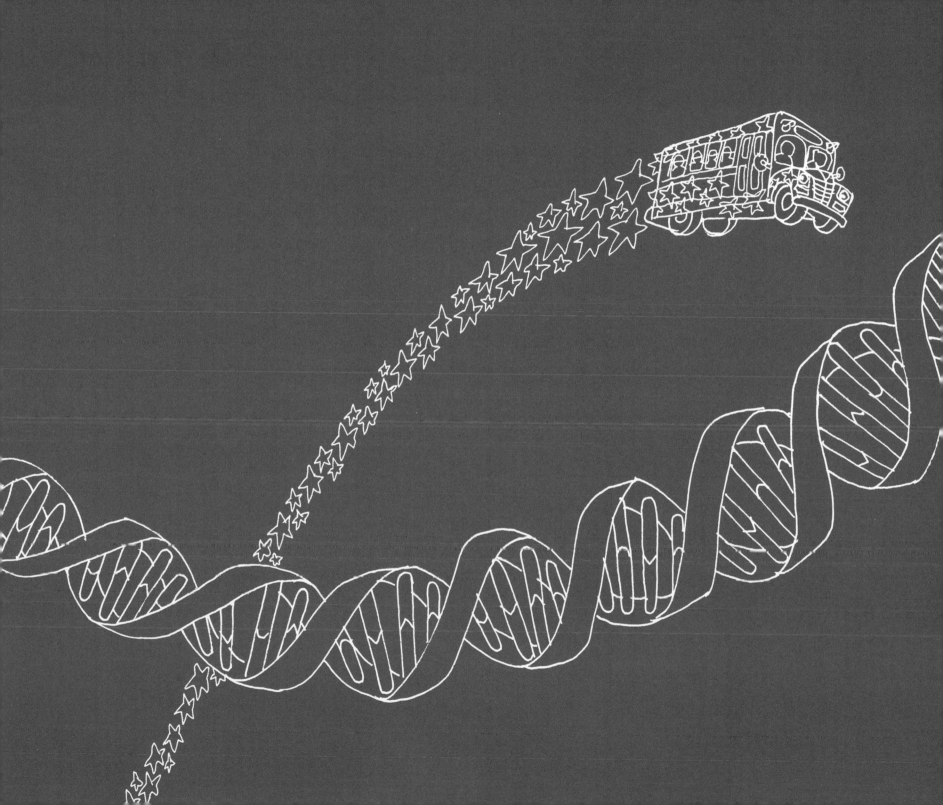

The Magic School Bus
Explores Human Evolution

By Joanna Cole

Illustrated by Bruce Degen

Scholastic Press / New York

The author and illustrator would like to thank
Catherine Badgley, Professor at the University of Michigan,
for her expert review, covering billions of years of evolution.

Library of Congress Cataloging-in-Publication Data Available

ISBN 978-0-590-10828-7

10 9 8 7 6 5 4 3 2 1   21 22 23 24 25

Printed in China   38
First edition, April 2021

The text type was set in 15-point Bookman Light.
The illustrations were created using pen and ink,
watercolor, color pencil, and gouache.

CHARLES DARWIN SAILED
ON *THE BEAGLE*

GALÁPAGOS TORTOISE

For my grandchildren,
Annabelle and William Helms,
with love. — J.C.

To all our readers,
around the world and here at home,
who have traveled with us. — B.D.

Have you met our teacher, Ms. Frizzle?
Have you seen her strange dresses and her
strange shoes?
Have you noticed her weird school bus?
If you have, you probably know that
anything can happen in Ms. Frizzle's
class—and it usually does!

RUBBER TREE

WE GO ON WACKY CLASS TRIPS.

WHAT DO YOU MEAN—WACKY?

STICK AROUND, BO. YOU'LL SEE.

ANIMAL CELL

PLANT CELL

Today we were making family trees. Wanda's was the longest. Ralphie's was the funniest. Arnold's was the shortest.

8

"I wish I'd found more of my ancestors," said Arnold.
Ms. Frizzle got that funny look in her eye.
"That wish just might come true, Arnold," she said.
"To the bus, kids!"

WE'LL SEE THE FAMILY TREE OF THE WHOLE HUMAN RACE!

A TRIP? I DIDN'T MEAN IT! I TAKE IT BACK!

NO BACKSIES, ARNOLD.

HOW OLD IS THE EARTH?
by Alex
Scientists have found out that the Earth is very, very, very, very, very, very, very, very, very, very, very, very old.

I'M FOUR AND A HALF BILLION YEARS OLD.

GOSH, WE ARE ONLY TWO.

PEPPER AND PAPRIKA—CLASS GUINEA PIGS

9

WHAT IS EVOLUTION?
by Phoebe
Evolution is change over time.
All living things evolved, or developed, from earlier life-forms. This happened very, very slowly.

HOW DO WE KNOW EVOLUTION IS TRUE?
by Tim
One way is by studying fossils — the remains of living things from long ago. Fossils show how one kind of animal or plant changed as time went on.

EOHIPPUS | MESOHIPPUS | MERYCHIPPUS | PLIOHIPPUS | MODERN HORSE

As soon as we got on the bus, a new road appeared behind our school.
That was weird enough, but then Ms. Frizzle started to drive down the road backward.

Back

WE'RE GOING BACK THREE AND A HALF BILLION YEARS!

ARE WE THERE YET?

GOING BACK

New Road

"We're backing up in time, kids," she said.
"We'll be the first class to see human evolution."

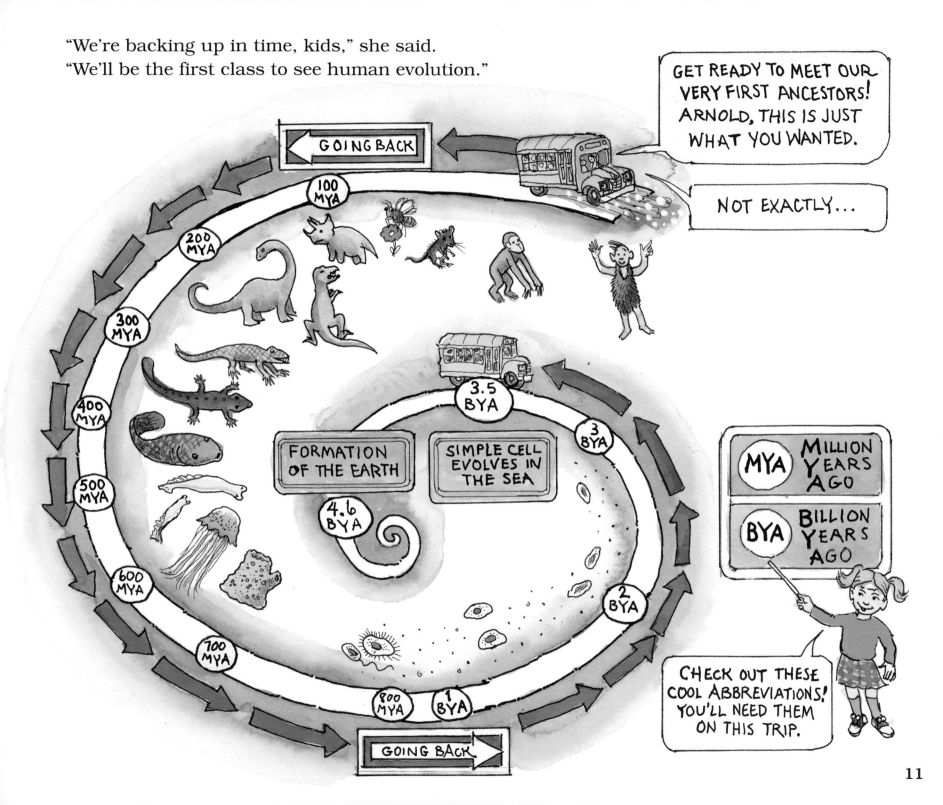

WHAT ARE CELLS?
by Wanda
Cells are tiny living things.
They are so small we need
a microscope to see them.
Inside the cell are parts
that work together
to keep the cell alive
and healthy.

SINGLE-CELL ORGANISM

Some cells live
on their own.

Others make up the
bodies of larger
plants and animals.

PLANT CELL

This plant has
millions of cells.

"The first life began in the sea," Dorothy Ann read from her book. "The first living things were tiny cells."
The bus doors opened, and we tumbled out underwater. Suddenly we were wearing strange costumes—we told you our class trips were weird.

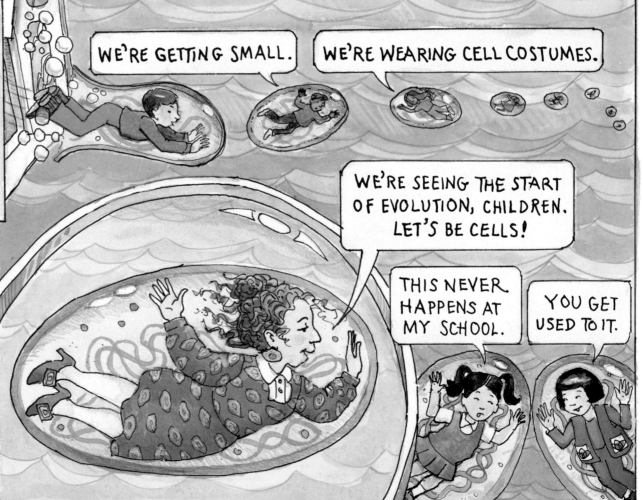

12

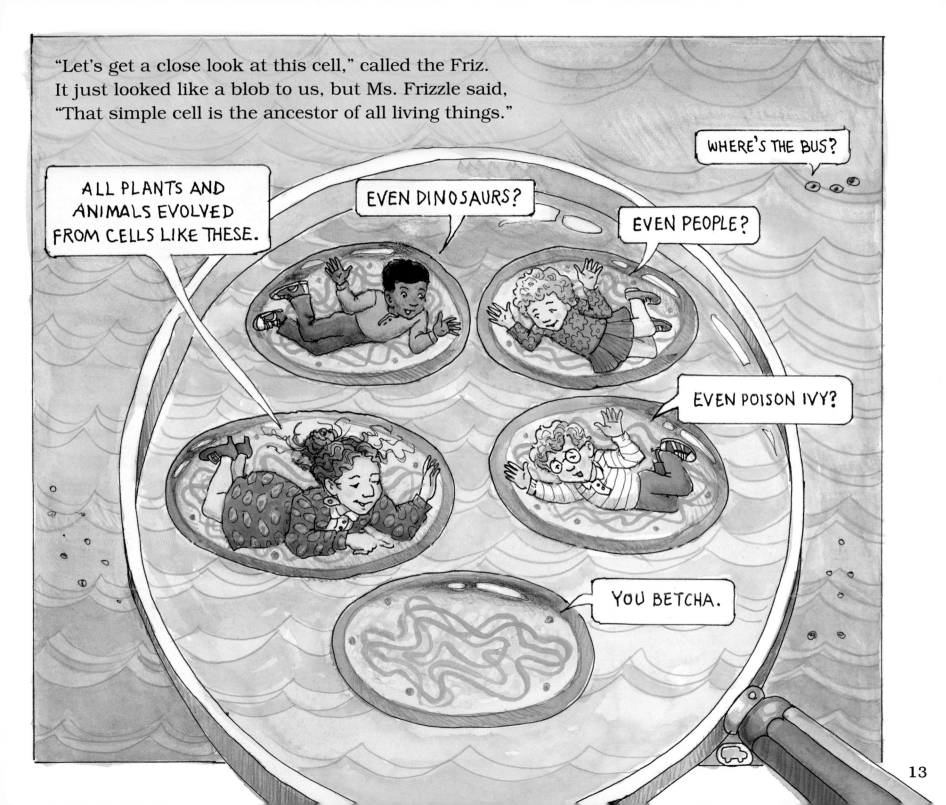

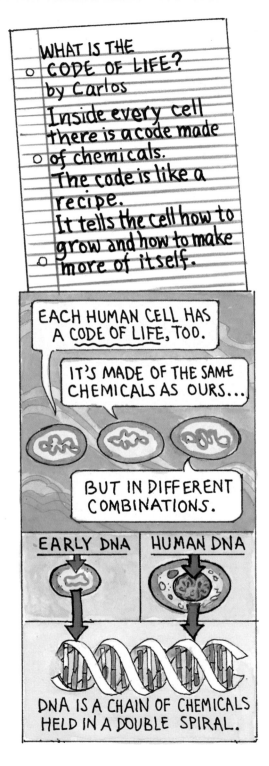

"Notice the stuff inside the cell," said the Friz.
"It's the code of life—also known as DNA."
We were noticing the DNA, when all of a sudden
Tim exclaimed, "Look at the cell!"
"It's splitting in half!" yelped Ralphie.

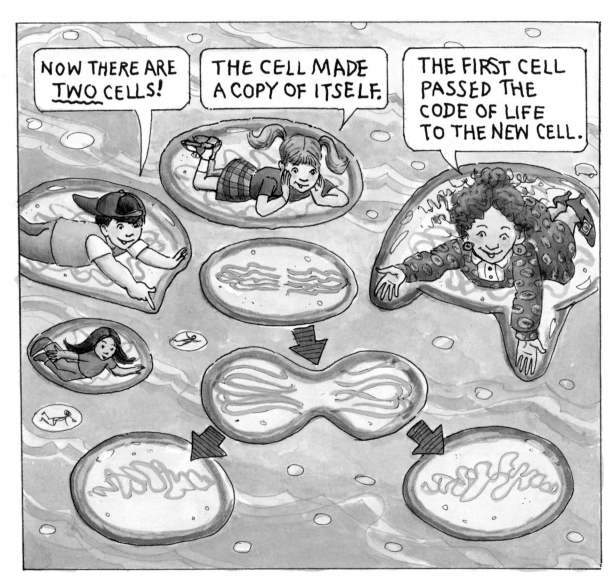

A FABULOUS NEW CELL
by Tim

The old simple cell has only a few parts. The complex cell has many parts.

> I HAVE WAY MORE PARTS THAN YOU.

SIMPLE	COMPLEX

ALL HUMAN CELLS ARE COMPLEX
by Phoebe

This new cell is the first step to more complex life-forms—like us. Every cell in the human body has many parts.

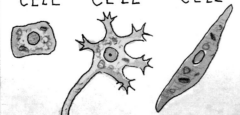

SKIN CELL   NERVE CELL   MUSCLE CELL

Big cells had been eating little cells for a lo-o-o-ong time. Sometimes when a little cell was eaten, it was not digested. Instead, it became a working part of the big cell. Ms. Frizzle said the big cell was now a complex cell. We looked like complex cells now, too.

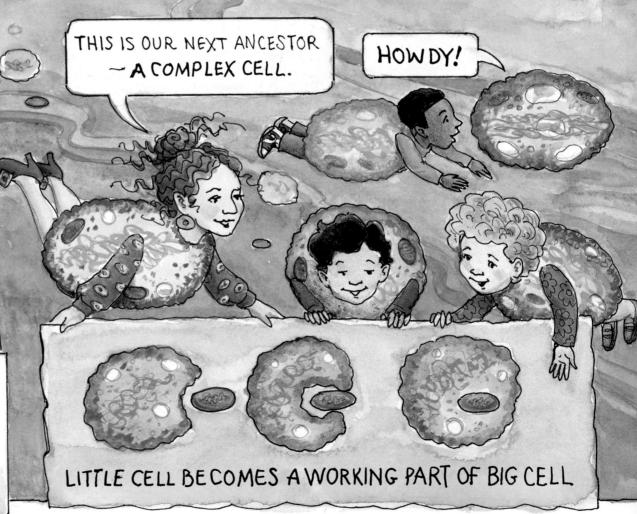

> THIS IS OUR NEXT ANCESTOR ~ A COMPLEX CELL.

> HOWDY!

LITTLE CELL BECOMES A WORKING PART OF BIG CELL

17

We traveled forward millions of years and found our next ancestor. "Many cells have clumped together to make a new animal," said our teacher. "It's a tiny sponge. It's the first animal to have many cells."

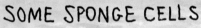

HOW HUMANS ARE LIKE SPONGES
by Arnold
Sponges have many cells.
Humans do, too.

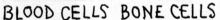

HOW WE ARE DIFFERENT
A sponge has about a dozen different kinds of cells. A human has 200 different kinds of cells.

SOME SPONGE CELLS

SOME HUMAN CELLS
HEART CELLS   SKIN CELLS

BLOOD CELLS   BONE CELLS

EACH SPONGE IS ACTUALLY THE SIZE OF THIS DOT.

SPONGE ANCHORED TO A ROCK

"Follow the Friz, everyone!" yelled Ralphie.
We went forward many millions of years.
There had been many changes in DNA
over the years.
A new animal had evolved—a jellyfish.
It had tentacles.
Guess what? We did, too.

I FEEL SO SLIMY!

DON'T DAWDLE, CHILDREN. WE HAVE ALMOST 630 MILLION YEARS TO GO.

HOW HUMANS ARE LIKE JELLYFISH
by Wanda
o Jellyfish have many kinds of cells.
o The cells are organized into parts that do different jobs.
Human cells are like that, too.
o

HOW WE ARE DIFFERENT
o We have trillions more cells than jellyfish.
We have a brain and a backbone.
o Jellyfish do not.

YOU'RE SPINELESS!

SO ARE YOU!

NERVE NET (NO BRAIN)

MOUTH ON UNDERSIDE

STINGING TENTACLES

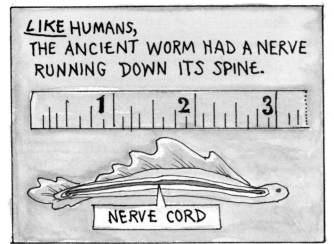

LIKE HUMANS,
THE ANCIENT WORM HAD A NERVE RUNNING DOWN ITS SPINE.

NERVE CORD

Going forward again, we met a tiny sea worm. "The sea worm is the first animal with the beginning of a backbone!" said the Friz. "Isn't it wonderful, Arnold?" she added. "We're back when worms ruled the world!"

WE'RE WORMS?

I'M GOING TO CHOP THIS BRANCH OFF MY FAMILY TREE.

450 MILLION YEARS AGO

Millions of years went by, and life kept changing. There were still sea worms, but jawless fish had evolved, too.

These fish had skeletons, and they ate by sucking gross stuff from the ocean floor.

We said, "Yuck," but the Friz said this was a big step toward human beings.

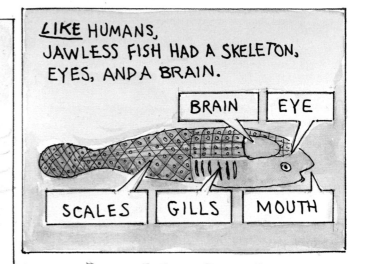

LIKE HUMANS, JAWLESS FISH HAD A SKELETON, EYES, AND A BRAIN.

BRAIN EYE SCALES GILLS MOUTH

FIRST PLANTS ON LAND: GREEN ALGAE.
NO LAND ANIMALS YET.

Where we are now

450 MYA

YOU'LL NEVER BELIEVE WHAT HAPPENED TO FISH OVER THE NEXT 65 MILLION YEARS!

WHO WOULD BELIEVE WHAT HAPPENS TO US ON CLASS TRIPS?

21

LIKE HUMANS, RAY-FINS HAD JAWS AND TEETH.

FIN BONES FANNED OUT LIKE RAYS.

ON LAND: BY THIS TIME THERE WERE PLANTS, MITES, MILLIPEDES, AND SCORPIONS.

We went forward to a time when there were ray-finned fish.
The thin bones in their fins spread out, like rays.
That made the fish good at swimming.
These fish also had jaws and sharp teeth.
That made them good at eating.

BO! LOOK AT THAT FISH SWIM!

LOOK AT IT BITE!

WE'RE FINALLY MAKING A SPLASH IN THE WORLD!

WHAT WERE THE BENEFITS OF GOING ON LAND?
by Molly

- There was a lot of food just waiting to be eaten.
- There were no predators yet, so it was safer to be on land than to be in water.

WATER—
REALLY BIG PREDATORS

LAND—
NO BIG PREDATORS YET

Ten million years later, life had changed a lot, which meant animals' DNA had changed a lot, too.
We saw fish with legs! They still had gills like fish, but they had nostrils and lungs, too.

LAND HO!

AT LAST!

WE ARE HALF-FISH AND HALF-LAND ANIMAL.

CAN WE GO, TOO?

NO, TODAY IS A SCHOOL DAY FOR LITTLE FISH.

24

SCORPION

The fish with legs couldn't walk all the way onto the land, but they could crawl and prop themselves up on their front legs. They even had wrists to help with that. Their legs were stronger than ever.

LIKE HUMANS, FISH WITH LEGS HAD LIMBS WITH ONE UPPER BONE AND TWO LOWER BONES, AND WRISTS.

UPPER ARM BONE

LOWER ARM BONES

WRIST

FISH WITH LEGS | HUMAN

Where we are now

375 MYA

LOOK AT ALL THE STUFF TO EAT!

WE COULD HAVE CRUNCHY SCORPIONS AND JUICY CENTIPEDES.

UH, I THINK I'LL SAVE ROOM FOR DESSERT.

CENTIPEDE

CRAWL THIS WAY, CLASS.

25

REPTILES OF TODAY

LIZARDS

SNAKES

TURTLES

CROCODILES AND ALLIGATORS

ALL EVOLVED LATER

295 MILLION YEARS AGO
EARLY REPTILES

As we went forward in time, there were still amphibians.
But our next ancestor was a new kind of animal—a reptile.
Reptile eggs had a waterproof shell to keep moisture in.
Now the babies could hatch on land!

WE CAN LIVE ON LAND!

LIKE, IN HOUSES?

THAT COMES LATER...

...MUCH LATER.

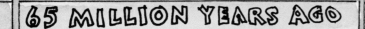

65 MILLION YEARS AGO

Most mammals were little creatures.
By day, they hid from the dinosaurs.
At night, they came out to hunt for food.
Some scurried under bushes.
Others climbed trees and hid in the leaves.

CHOMP

STOMP

YUCK!

Then the dinosaurs went extinct.
But mammals survived.

FLOWERING PLANTS

THIS IS OUR BIG CHANCE! LET'S EVOLVE!

NO MORE DINOS!

TO MORE AND MORE MAMMALS

WHAT ARE PRIMATES?
by Phil
Primates are mammals that have:
- Eyes that face forward.
- Grasping hands and (usually) grasping feet.
- Nails on fingers and toes (instead of claws).
- Bigger brains than other animals of the same size.

PRIMATES OF TODAY

LEMURS TARSIERS

MONKEYS APES

AND HUMANS

ALL EVOLVED LATER

55 MILLION YEARS AGO

Only ten million years later, our next ancestors had evolved in tropical forests. They were primates. They were different from the earliest mammals. Like humans, their eyes faced front, not to the sides. That helped them judge distances, so they didn't miss a branch and fall when they climbed trees.

LOOK! THEY'RE EATING FRUIT AND NUTS.

AT LEAST IT'S NOT MORE BUGS!

THAT'S DESSERT!

The evolution of primates that led
to humans happened in Africa.
The primates split into branches.
The monkeys went one way.
The apes went another.

The apes were bigger and heavier than
monkeys, and they didn't have tails.
Their brains were bigger.

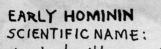

EARLY HOMININ
SCIENTIFIC NAME:
Australopithecus afarensis

- BRAIN IS A LITTLE BIGGER THAN A CHIMP'S.
- USES STICKS AND ROCKS AS TOOLS.
- EATS MOSTLY FRUIT AND LEAVES.
- ARMS ARE LONGER THAN LEGS (WHICH IS GOOD FOR CLIMBING).

ARE WE APES...

...OR HUMANS?

A LITTLE OF BOTH.

By five million years ago, *amazing* new animals had evolved.
Ms. Frizzle called them hominins.
They were still good at climbing like apes, but their feet, legs, and hips had changed.
They could walk upright, so their hands were free to do things.

WE CAN WORK WITH OUR HANDS.

WE CAN CARRY THINGS.

NOT THIS MANY THINGS!

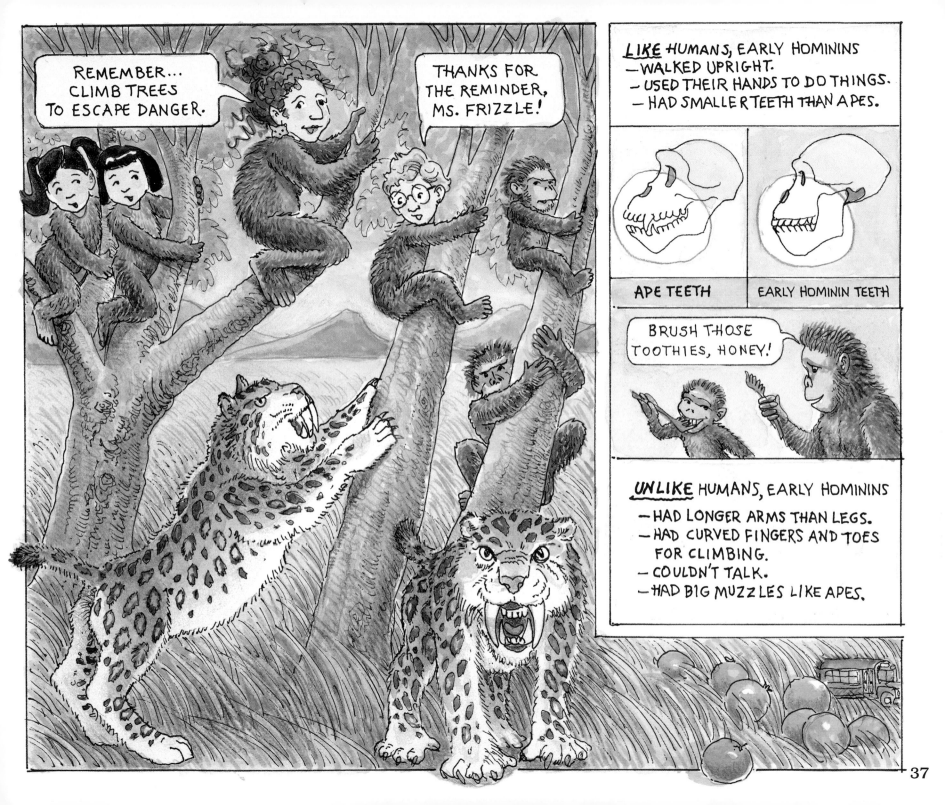

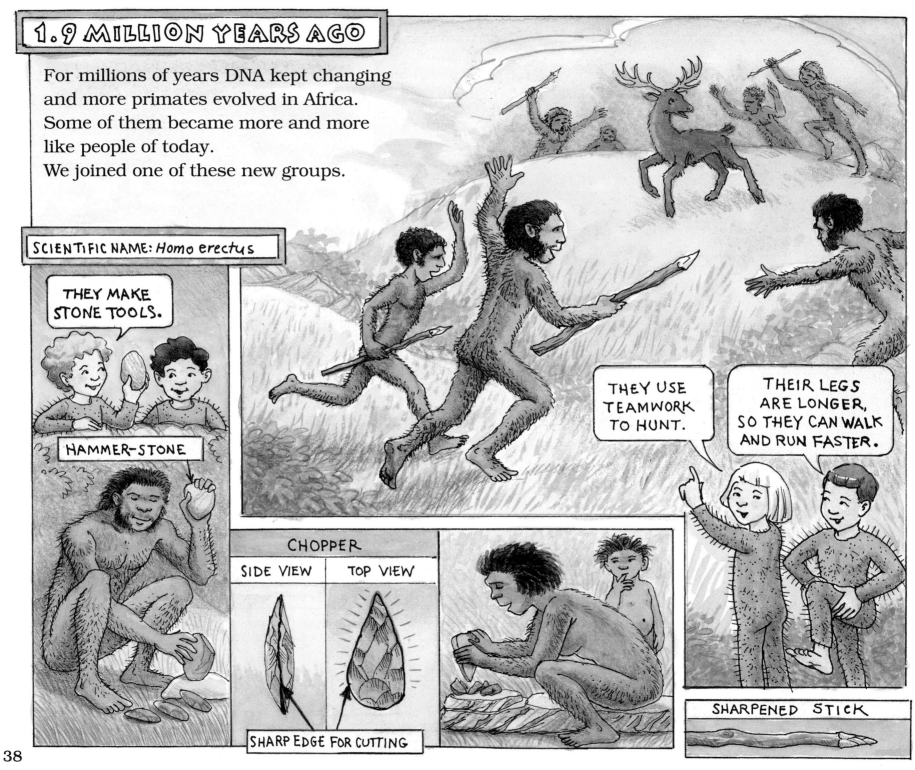

WHAT FOSSIL SKULLS SHOW US: A BIGGER, MORE COMPLEX BRAIN EVOLVED OVER TIME.

SKULL · BRAINCASE				
APE	Australopithecus afarensis	Homo erectus	Homo heidelbergensis	Homo sapiens

TURN THE PAGE FOR MORE ON Homo sapiens ⇨

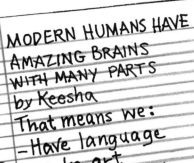

MODERN HUMANS HAVE AMAZING BRAINS WITH MANY PARTS
by Keesha
That means we:
- Have language
- Make art
- Solve hard problems
- Invent incredible things

THINKING, PLANNING

MEMORY, LANGUAGE

WE EVOLVED IN AFRICA
by Rachel
People used to think that the first modern humans arose in Europe about 45,000 years ago.
But now scientists have found evidence showing that modern humans lived in Africa long before that.

Around 160,000 years ago, *Homo sapiens* evolved.
They were human beings.
They could talk. They could think.
They could learn. Just like you and me.

SCIENTIFIC NAME: *Homo sapiens*

WE ARE ALL *HOMO SAPIENS*!

HELLO!

I made this.

Does that mean *Hello*?

Now we need more fruit.

WEARING ORNAMENTS: BEADS MADE FROM SHELLS

TALKING AND PLANNING

41

DIGESTING MILK:
WHERE HUMANS MILKED COWS, GOATS, OR REINDEER, PEOPLE EVOLVED WHO CAN DIGEST MILK AS ADULTS.
(ORIGINALLY, ONLY BABIES COULD DO THAT.)

LIGHT SKIN:
WHERE THE SUN WAS WEAKER, SKIN COLOR BECAME LIGHTER. (THAT MADE IT EASIER FOR SKIN TO MAKE VITAMIN D WITH SUNLIGHT.)

PEOPLE TOOK THE THINGS THEY LEARNED AND MADE IN AFRICA TO OTHER PLACES.

Tens of thousands of years ago, small bands of humans left Africa.
They traveled to new places and made new homes there.
In the new places, human bodies evolved in different ways.
But Ms. Frizzle said these changes are small.
In all the important ways, our bodies and minds are alike.

OUTSIDE OF AFRICA: SOME MODERN HUMANS HAD BABIES WITH EARLIER HUMANS CALLED NEANDERTHALS AND DENISOVANS. BOTH OF THOSE GROUPS DIED OUT ABOUT 30,000 YEARS AGO. BUT TODAY SOME OF US HAVE A SMALL AMOUNT OF THEIR DNA.

STOCKY BODIES:
IN SOME COLD PLACES, BODIES BECAME SHORTER AND THICKER. (IT WAS BETTER FOR KEEPING HEAT IN.)

DARK SKIN AGAIN:
WHEN PEOPLE TRAVELED TO NEW PLACES WHERE THE SUN WAS STRONG, DARKER SKIN EVOLVED AGAIN.

We had not seen our school bus for almost the entire trip.
Now—surprise!—it showed up.
We hopped on and started traveling.

As the years went by, humans spread all over the world. They created different cultures in the different places they settled down.

Ms. Frizzle said, "We may speak different languages, eat different food, make different art, and have different religions. But we are all human beings with the same family tree."

Ms. Frizzle kept her foot on the gas pedal, and we didn't stop anywhere else. We waved good-bye to people all over the world and headed back to school.

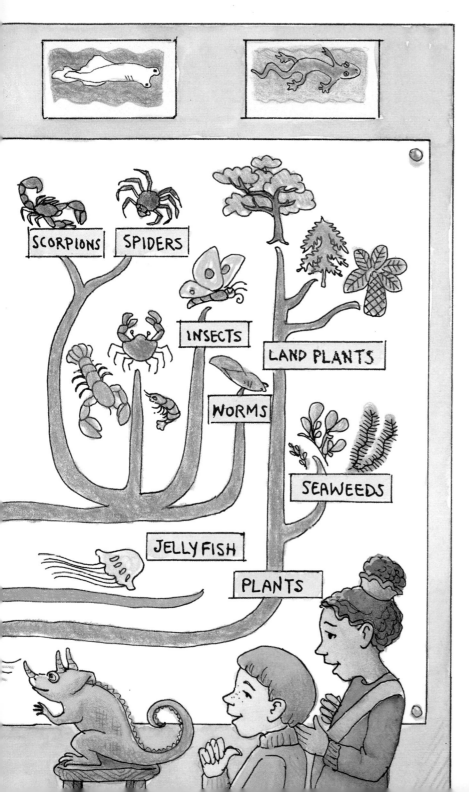

SCORPIONS SPIDERS

INSECTS

LAND PLANTS

WORMS

SEAWEEDS

JELLY FISH

PLANTS

After that trip, we knew the story of our species and where we came from.
The next question was, "Where are we going?"
We didn't know the answer, because with
Ms. Frizzle for a teacher, it's always a surprise.

MY BROTHER'S CLASS WENT TO THE MUSEUM.

OUR CLASS IS DIFFERENT.

VERY DIFFERENT.

IMPORTANT SCHOOL RULES

1. Classes do not have permission to go back in time. (Rule broken on page 11.)

2. Class guinea pigs may not speak during school hours. (Note bad behavior on page 9.)

3. Simple cells are not allowed to talk at any time. (See pages 13–14.)

4. Students may *never* climb trees without a parent or guardian's consent. (See pages 32–34 and 37.)

5. Teachers are not authorized to cook meat over an open fire. (See page 39.)

6. On Mondays through Fridays, students may not travel around the world. (See pages 44–45.)

THE EVIDENCE FOR EVOLUTION
How We Know Evolution Happens

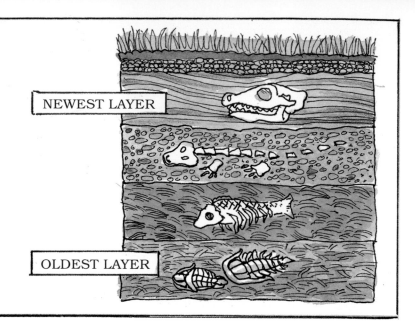

NEWEST LAYER

OLDEST LAYER

ROCKS TELL THE STORY

The Earth is made up of layers of rock. The older, deeper rocks have fossils of simple living things. As the rocks get newer, there are new, more complex fossils. This tells us that life evolved over time.

LINKED TOGETHER

There are many series of fossils that follow one another like links in a chain. These chains show how certain animals evolved.

FINS TO FEET

BODY PLANS

Even animals that look very different from each other have bones and body parts that are similar. This suggests that the animals are related to each other, that they do not have a completely separate evolution.

HORSE

LION

BEGINNING BABIES

When babies first start growing in the egg or in the womb, they are called embryos. At first, embryos of different animals are so much alike that it can be hard to tell them apart.

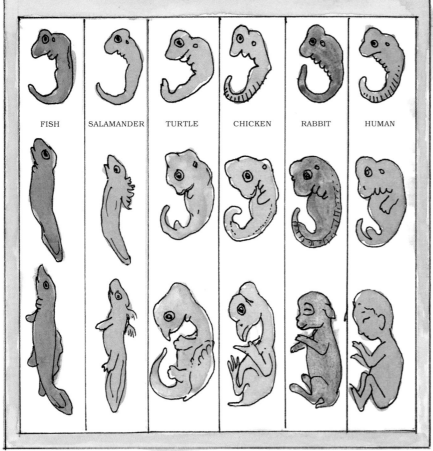

FISH   SALAMANDER   TURTLE   CHICKEN   RABBIT   HUMAN

THE CODE OF LIFE

Our DNA is made of the same ingredients as all other living things—including bacteria, bananas, cats, dogs, and apes.

The code of life is shaped like two spirals—called a double helix. It is similar in animals and plants. The thing that is different, that makes a living being unique, is the order of the chemicals (or ingredients) in the code.

LEFTOVERS

Animals sometimes have leftover parts that are of no use to them, but these parts show their ancestry. For instance, whales of today have tiny leg bones inside their bodies. This shows that they evolved from animals that walked on land.

IT'S HAPPENING NOW
Evolution is still at work!

 Bacteria and viruses evolve to resist medicines.

 Weeds become immune to weed killers.

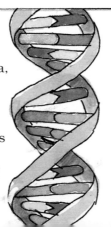 Mosquitoes and other pests evolve so poisons no longer kill them.

People have to try to invent new ways to fight the new germs and pests.

HOW DOES EVOLUTION WORK?

NATURAL SELECTION MEANS NATURE CHOOSES

CHARLES DARWIN EXPLAINED IT

Darwin was a scientist who lived more than 100 years ago. He wrote a famous book that said evolution works by a process called *NATURAL SELECTION*.

1. There were some mice that lived on a beach with white sand.

2. The mice were light colored and dark colored.

3. Hawks could not see the light-colored mice well against the white sand.

4. After a while, almost all the mice were light.

5. Nearby was a beach with black sand. Some mice went there.

6. At that beach, hawks killed the lighter mice. The darker ones escaped more often.

7. Darker mice passed on their color to their babies. In time, most of the mice on that beach were dark.

This process is called natural selection because nature selects, or chooses, which living things survive to pass on their traits to their babies. The hawks and the black sand didn't really choose for more of the darker mice to survive. It happened naturally, because the lighter mice were easier to catch.

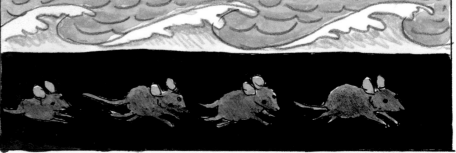

PEOPLE MAKE SELECTIONS, TOO

Unlike in nature, when people select for differences, they do it on purpose.

Suppose a farmer wants cows that give more milk. She chooses the best milkers to breed.

Some of those cows' babies grow up to give more milk.

By breeding the best milkers over time, the farmer ends up with a herd that gives more milk.

By using selection, breeders create different kinds of animals and plants.

Just look at these chickens— all from the same ancestor.

A plant breeder has selected for different colors of flowers.

The first dogs evolved from wolves. Later, people selected dogs for different traits, and now we have dogs of all shapes and sizes.